Toward a Free Society
A Short Guide on Building a Culture of Liberty

Skyler J. Collins

Everything-Voluntary.com

Published 2015 by Skyler J. Collins
Visit: www.skylerjcollins.com

Cover design by KindleBookeCovers.com

ISBN-13: 978-1508419167
ISBN-10: 1508419167

To my wife, children, and all who value liberty.

CONTENTS

Preface   i

1   Introduction   1

2   Parenting   6

3   Schooling   13

4   Radical Unschooling   18

5   Agorism   25

6   Moral Outrage   32

     Further Reading   39

     About the Author   41

PREFACE

This isn't my first publication, but it is my first publication that I authored entirely. *Everything Voluntary: From Politics to Parenting* was self-published in 2012, myself as editor. It was an anthology of essays introducing the philosophy of voluntaryism in politics, the economy, parenting, and childhood education.[1] These are also the areas covered here, again self-published.

This booklet was originally written at the beginning of 2015 as a series of columns on my website, Everything-Voluntary.com, where I write and podcast weekly. I decided to make it available in paperback and the various digital formats.

---

[1] Available in several formats at http://skyler.link/evcbook1

I hope that what you read here proves enlightening. I highly recommend that as you encounter the footnotes, you take the time to access the recommended material. This guide would not be complete without the reader taking full advantage of what it has to offer. Likewise, the "further reading" at the end will help you increase your understanding of the practical applications of the themes I cover.

I am forever indebted to the countless individuals that have had an impact on my thinking throughout my life. My life and the culture of my family have been immeasurably improved by what I have discovered, absorbed, and applied. I am not the same man I was ten years ago, five years ago, or even one year ago. I'm a better person, a better husband, a better father, and a better friend. And I am quite certain that I still have a long way to go before I'll be the person my loved ones deserve. Please, enjoy this booklet, and if you do, pass it on.

1 INTRODUCTION

A free society, where liberty is secure, is necessarily one where you'll find the widespread observance of the voluntary principle (all human relations should happen voluntarily, or not all).[2] Of course, not everyone is required to practice voluntaryism[3], but enough must so that society remains free, a state of affairs demanded by our psychological needs. Good and well. But how do we achieve a free society? What are the prerequisites? The antecedents? Before we'll have widespread liberty, we must build a culture of

---

[2] Read "The Voluntary Principle" by the author at http://skyler.link/evcprinciple

[3] Read "The Philosophy of Voluntaryism" by the author at http://skyler.link/evcphilosophy

liberty. How are cultures built? We aren't born with a culture. That's a process that occurs over our lifetimes, beginning at birth. Enculturation, socialization, and education are the antecedents for every kind of society we can imagine or observe. When it comes to liberty, it seems best secured through a popular feeling of moral outrage toward its denial. How do we accomplish that? We'll explore what I consider to be a very good answer in this booklet, beginning with definitions.

Definitions

Liberty is when one is "free from restraint" by another.[4] Imposing your will by force onto others is to deny them liberty. The authority to deny a person their liberty must either be granted by that person, or obtained as a result of that person initiating the use of force against others. The authority to retaliate by force to another's initiation of force is granted by virtue of their obvious belief that the initiation of force is a valid human interaction. Liberty, then, is the natural state of every person, and its denial must be justified on the aforementioned grounds.[5]

---

[4] Read "Liberty, Freedom, and Power" by the author at http://skyler.link/evclibertyfreedom

[5] Read "Punishment and Proportionality" by Stephan Kinsella at http://skyler.link/misesestoppel (PDF)

Enculturation is the "gradual acquisition of the characteristics and norms of a culture or group by a person" not yet enculturated.[6] As people grow from babies into adults, they are introduced to the various practices of their family's culture. They learn to value certain aspects of culture, things like social organization, customs and traditions, language, art and literature, forms of government, economic systems, and religion.

Socialization is "the lifelong process of inheriting and disseminating norms, customs and ideologies, providing an individual with the skills and habits necessary for participating within his or her own society."[7] Similar to enculturation, socialization is how one learns to get along and cooperate with others around him, others who may or may not share one's culture.

Moral outrage is a feeling of disgust and/or anger "to infringements or transgressions on what people perceive to be the immunities they, or others with whom they identify, can expect on the basis of their rights and privileges and what they understand to be their reasonable expectations

---

[6] See the Wikipedia entry for "Enculturation" at http://skyler.link/wikienculturation

[7] See the Wikipedia entry for "Socialization" at http://skyler.link/wikisocialization

regarding the behavior of others."[8] One's socialization will determine what is considered the immunities, rights, and privileges of different groups or classes of people, their violation of which produces the feeling of moral outrage. As it stands, the possibility of moral outrage is a result of one's socialization and enculturation.

Education is the process of receiving "a body of knowledge" and wisdom, the latter a result of the application of our knowledge through experience.[9] As we learn new things, we naturally try to fit them in to what we've learned before, building for ourselves an academic tapestry from which to evaluate the socialization and enculturation that is always occurring within us. Through education, we experience re-socialization and re-enculturation, which will lead to a change in the list of behaviors by others that will cause us to feel moral outrage, as well as the list of behaviors that won't.

Having given detailed definitions of the preceding terms, I will now use them throughout the remainder of this booklet. We'll first look at

---

[8] Read "Moral Outrage: Territoriality in Human Guise" by Ward H. Goodenough at http://skyler.link/whgmo (PDF)
[9] See the Wikipedia entry for "Education" at http://skyler.link/wikieducation

parenting, followed by schooling. And then we'll look at building a culture of liberty through radical unschooling and agorism, broadly applied. I'll finish this booklet on the topic of "moral outrage" and why this is a key component for achieving a free society.

2 PARENTING

Having thus defined our terms, we can begin exploring the necessary prerequisites to building a culture of liberty, and ultimately, a free society. We must start at the same place where each if us began life, the home. Our parents are first to influence our enculturation and socialization, followed by our siblings, grandparents, cousins, friends, and so forth.

Attachment Parenting

Parenting science in the realm of attachment theory posits that our ability to empathize with others begins its development in infancy.[10]

---

[10] Read "Observations on Attachment Parenting Outcomes" by Dr. Sears at http://skyler.link/searsapoutcomes

Mother/baby eye contact and bonding is the first step. From there, breastfeeding, babywearing, and cosleeping continue the process. Empathy is important if we are to make sense of the plight of others. Feeling moral outrage toward someone being violated is as important for the desire to secure their rights as it is our own.[11] Following attachment parenting practices is the first step toward building a culture of liberty.[12]

Children's Rights

The second is the practice of respecting a child's self-ownership and property rights.[13] "The rights of children" is an oft-debated topic among libertarians, but as I hope to show here, irrelevant to the need to socialize them to expect their rights be respected once they've entered adulthood. If little people will one day be big people, and we want them to consider themselves as self-owners having the right to own and trade property, then we should socialize them as self-owners having property rights throughout their entire life.

---

[11] Read "Rights are a Tool" by the author at http://skyler.link/evcrightstool

[12] See the Natural Child Project's attachment parenting article archive at http://skyler.link/ncpaparchive

[13] Read "How We Came to Own Ourselves" by Stephan Kinsella at http://skyler.link/misesownourselves

As self-owners with property rights, all the mainstream parenting practices that include arbitrary consequences to either "good" or "bad" behavior go right out the window. Why? Because arbitrary consequences are disrespectful to the child's rights (spanking and time-outs are acts of aggression). Think about it. Because children are ignorant (without knowledge and wisdom, or uneducated) and still early in the socialization process, they make many mistakes, which include, among other things, the handling of their big emotions. As self-owners with property rights, children must be met where they're at. They have a right to feel the things they feel, and to make the mistakes they make.[14] Their mistakes are evidence of their ignorance. What they need so that they make less mistakes, is more honest knowledge and wisdom.

Natural Consequences

Arbitrary consequences are educational, sure, but because they are arbitrary, they do not convey honest knowledge and wisdom regarding the particular mistake being corrected. Rather, they convey dishonest knowledge and wisdom. For

---

[14] Read "Emotions are Not Bad Behavior" by Robin Grille at http://skyler.link/ncprgemotions

example, when a child steals a toy from another child, his mistake is being the cause of hurt in the child whose toy he stole. That child is not only hurt, but also less trusting and more resentful of the first child. Those are the natural consequences of stealing someone's stuff. It's even possible, and natural, for the second child to feel anger and desire to use his power to take back his toy and attempt revenge.

The correction that the first child needs is to be made aware of how his actions negatively affected someone else, and all the fallout from that. This is an honest approach to the child. Alternatively, when a parent offers an arbitrary consequence, what the child learns as natural cause and effect is wrong.[15] He learns not that stealing causes pain in others and their resentment toward him, but rather that stealing causes his own pain and resentment from him toward his parent. He's thus been defrauded out of a genuine and honest learning experience through the use of arbitrary consequences. His rights have been disrespected because he's been attacked by his parent, given fraudulent information, and now expected to act in accordance with a lie. He's been

---

[15] Read "Why Do We Hurt Our Children?" by James Kimmell at http://skyler.link/evcwhyhurtchildren

set up to fail, in other words, and to take that failure, and every failure compounded after that, into the future, with less of an expectation of having his self-ownership and property rights respected by others, and more of a willingness to violate the self-ownership or property rights of others. And more, he's socialized into the belief that his parents have a greater right to enact arbitrary consequences and to handle him than his right to experience natural consequences and choose how he'll be handled by others. This bodes poorly for building a culture of liberty.

Misbehavior

A better approach for socializing liberty than the use of arbitrary consequences is to recognize that every mistake a child makes is the result of some need not being met. I no longer believe that children "misbehave", rather, they behave exactly as I would expect given their needs and their ignorance in meeting them properly.[16] They do the best they can under the circumstances. In the example above, the first child has a genuine need to explore the toy being played with by someone else. Had he enough knowledge and wisdom, he'd

---

[16] Read "Children Don't Really Misbehave" by Thomas Gordon at http://skyler.link/ncptgmisbehave

know that he should either wait for it to be free or persuade the other child to part with it. But because he's still ignorant, he does the next best thing (from his perspective), he takes it. The natural consequences as described above are the result. The first child, if he is to survive in society and maintain his life and liberty, needs to learn about these consequences so that he's more likely to value cooperation (over domination) in the future. He learns through being made aware of them by either a parent or the natural course of events. But the parent's job is not done there.

The child also needs to learn how best to meet his need to explore the toys being explored by others. He needs to learn both how and why to cooperate. And he'll only learn these things if they are taught to him in the proper way for his age. As already explained, arbitrary consequences are always improper if we want our children to learn the value of cooperation, which those of us who value liberty, do. Instead, we should learn how to be effective listeners or discerners of, and communicators to, our children while fully respecting their self-ownership and property rights. The two programs - at the very least - that I recommend be studied by every parent who desires to live in a free society are Thomas Gordon's *Parent Effectiveness Training* [17] and Laura Markham's *Peaceful Parent, Happy Kids.* [18]

---

[17]Available in several formats at http://skyler.link/amznpet
[18]Available in several formats at http://skyler.link/amznpphk

3 SCHOOLING

Schooling is the typical next step in a person's life, and the socialization that occurs in school is quite ill-suited to building a culture of liberty. That's the intent, actually. Modern schooling was founded in Prussia as a means to socialize children into the acceptance of state authority (always illegitimate[19]) and a life of subservience to parents, opinion makers, educators, bureaucrats, and involuntary bosses.[20] The brilliance of schooling in this regard was not lost on the rest of the world's ruling class. It quickly spread to every country on

---

[19] Read "Why States are Illegitimate" by the author at http://skyler.link/evcillegitimate
[20] Read *Education: Free and Compulsory* by Murray Rothbard at http://skyler.link/misesmrefc

earth. Today, schooling is touted as a child's right and necessary for becoming a functional adult. But everything about school is antithetical to building a culture of liberty.

Unnatural Authority

To start, children are expected to obey adults who are emotional strangers to them. Teachers demand love, respect, and obedience without earning them the only way they can be earned, through bonding, connection, and impression.[21] And so, children learn to follow others because they said so, or else! The seeds of totalitarianism are thus planted, and watered with every "authority" the child encounters.[22] His life becomes one of obedience and regimentation.

Intellectual Prison

Children in school must do everything the person-in-charge tells them to do, whether they really want to or not, and often contrary to their own instincts. They must sit down and be quiet when they want to run around and be noisy. The must ask permission to get a tissue or go to the

---

[21] Read "Whence Cometh Respect?" by the author at http://skyler.link/evcrespect

[22] Read "Natural Law and Authority" by Michael Bakunin at http://skyler.link/evcauthority

bathroom. They must work on projects they might find uninteresting. When they do discover something interesting, the time they're allowed to focus on it is temporary and fleeting. Also, when they are presented with new information, it's presented in an unnatural way. Life does not approach us in subjects, nor does life separate facts from skills. Reading, writing, and arithmetic are skills. History, geography, and science are facts. Life has a way of throwing a big mess of experience (skills) and knowledge (facts) at us in a less than compartmentalized way. To approach learning unnaturally creates a handicap and, I believe, damages the desire to learn new things. I would call all of the above "intellectual prison" because of their non-intuitive and unnatural effects on the kind of education that children need to live in a free society, ie. freedom of thought and curiosity.[23]

Bullying

The prison metaphor certainly doesn't stop at the intellect, unfortunately. Children in school are forced to work all day in the classroom, and all evening at home. And when their work is unsatisfactory, they are punished. Not to mention

---

[23] Read "Why Don't Students Like School? Well, Duh…" by Peter Gray at http://skyler.link/ptpgwdsls

the punishing effect that rewards like stickers and grades have.[24] Alfie Kohn has explained the deleterious effects that grades have on the drive to learn and explore.[25] Artificial incentives cause people to put more focus on the incentive than on their work. The results are disinterest, short memory, and cheating. Another likely result is bullying. Some kids are made to feel stupid and ashamed of their poor performance in academics, a feeling that likely finds its relief in finding triumph on the playground, either in competitive sports, or in dominating those who they're compared against inside the classroom. Bullying is also a result of violent parenting.[26] This makes for improper socialization of both bullies and the bullied if the goal is a culture of liberty.[27]

For these and other reasons, including the pro-state "facts" that are disseminated, schooling is a

---

[24] Read *Punished by Rewards* by Alfie Kohn, available in several formats at http://skyler.link/amznrewards

[25] Read "The Case Against Grades" by Alfie Kohn at http://skyler.link/akgrades

[26] Read "Natural Born Bullies" by Robin Grille at http://skyler.link/evcbullies

[27] Read "The Long-Term Effects of Bullying on The Victim, the Bully, and the Bystander" by Rita Brhel at http://skyler.link/tafbullying

very bad place for children both as it regards their physical and intellectual needs and for the prospects of a free society.[28] Government schools are worse than private schools, which are worse than home schools. As I've written elsewhere, schooling is akin to prison, a plantation, and an indoctrination center.[29] The socialization that occurs in school is contrary to the socialization needed to achieve and maintain a free society. For that, our children need a radical approach to their education.

---

[28] Read *Weapons of Mass Instruction* by John Taylor Gatto, available in several formats at http://skyler.link/amzninstruction

[29] Read "Prison, Plantation, and Indoctrination Center" by the author at http://skyler.link/evcppic

4 RADICAL UNSCHOOLING

As shown in the previous chapter, schooling is an extremely poor practice for building a culture of liberty. Parents who've begun building that culture at home through attachment and peaceful discipline will find schooling to be a major counter-productive step in the socialization and enculturation of their children toward liberty.[30] Instead, such parents should educate themselves on the philosophy known as radical unschooling.[31] Not only does it meet the psychological and intellectual needs of children better than schooling,

---

[30] Read "The Trouble with Traditional Schooling" by Gregory Diehl at http://skyler.link/evctrouble
[31] Read "A Primer on Radical Unschooling" compiled by the author at http://skyler.link/evcunschooling

but it's also the best way to continue building a culture of liberty.[32]

Interest-led Learning

Unschooling is the philosophy that says that children learn best when they are focused on what interests them most.[33] Rather than following someone else's plan for learning, unschoolers are given the freedom to explore the world around them in their own way and on their own timescale. Both knowledge and wisdom are obtained as a matter of living joyfully alongside the necessary resources, which includes people, beginning but not ending with mom and dad, and things.[34] Unschoolers usually have unlimited access to the resources around them, which allows them to spend sufficient time learning or doing the things they find interesting. Because unschooled children are in complete control of their lives and their focus, they are naturally socialized into expecting such liberties in the future.[35] My own children

---

[32] Read *Free to Learn* by Peter Gray, available in several formats at http://skyler.link/amznfree2learn

[33] Read "The Unschooling Philosophy" by Pam Sorooshian at http://skyler.link/joyphilosophy

[34] Read "Living Joyfully: Unschooling" by Pam Laricchia at http://skyler.link/ljunschooling

[35] Read "Whatever They Want" by the author at http://skyler.link/evcwhatever

show remarkable assertiveness when the liberties they've been granted are being encroached.

Rules vs. Principles

What separates radical unschooling from unschooling is the former's focus on principles over rules. Rules are arbitrary and dictated, and may or may not be based on wisdom, but principles are a matter of reason and discovered through respectful dialogue and negotiation.[36] Going to bed at a certain time and place, eating all of one's food, doing chores on certain days, *et cetera*, are rules usually imposed on children by their parents. Contrary to rules like this, radical unschooling parents would discuss each of these things with their children, respectfully explaining why one should or shouldn't do this or that as it concerns each, and then let the child choose his own course of action.

For example, with bed times, mom and dad wouldn't assign a time for their kids to go to bed, but instead discuss with them any plans they have the next day, and what each person's needs are in keeping them.[37] Dad might have to work early, and

---

[36] Read "Living by Principles instead of by Rules" compiled by Sandra Dodd at http://skyler.link/doddrules

[37] Read "Sleeping" compiled by Sandra Dodd at http://skyler.link/doddsleeping

so needs to retire sooner than the rest of the family. And because dad needs a quiet house in order to get the sleep he needs to wake up on time for work (which finances everyone's lives and interests at the moment), he would appreciate it if everyone staying up could refrain from making too much noise. So long as this is all talked about respectfully, with willing consideration of everyone's needs, the family is likely to find an acceptable solution for all. Because radical unschoolers focus on principles rather than rules, children learn wisdom, negotiation, and respectful communication.[38] They also learn that their opinion matters and that they have a legitimate choice in the actions they take.

Natural Authority

When children have choice, have control, they learn something different about authority. Rather than authority being the person or persons who makes the rules that others must follow - or else! - authority is the person that can help others learn what they want to learn. Natural authority, in other words. Unschoolers discover all sorts of natural authorities throughout life as they explore and do

---

[38] Read "Living by Principles" compiled by Sandra Dodd at http://skyler.link/doddprinciples

interesting things. Nobody's born knowing everything, and so we must learn, and quite a bit of learning comes through the help of others. When others help us with our interests, our passions, they earn our respect and admiration as authorities in their field. Rather than being an arbitrary master, those who are considered "authority figures" are in actuality, servants. And any attempt at mastery over others is more likely seen as morally outrageous by those who've been socialized to view authorities in this way. Mom and dad included.[39]

Intellectual Freedom

Unlike those who are forced to go to school, unschoolers enjoy intellectual freedom, ie. freedom of the mind; the right to choose one's intellectual pursuits. Curiosity is one of humanity's greatest traits. It's unfortunately curtailed and often abolished through schooling, ie. educational compulsion. Anyone who's ever had kids will tell you how curious and fascinated about new things young children are.[40] This isn't something that's supposed to disappear as children get older. It only

---

[39] Read "Parental Authority" compiled by Sandra Dodd at http://skyler.link/doddauthority

[40] Read "Born to Explore" by Missy Willis at http://skyler.link/evcexplore

seems that way because schooling is the norm and people lose that natural drive to be curious and desire to learn new things when so much of their time and mental content is being forcefully prescribed by others. Those who maintain or re-discover their curiosity become the saviors of the world, those who invent new things and embark on new entrepreneurial ventures. The more people retain their natural curiosity, the harder it is to take away their liberties. And any attempt is more likely to be thwarted in creative ways.[41]

Respect

All of the above has the effect of creating genuine respect between adults and children. Respect is earned as a matter of the bonding that occurs between individuals. Bonding requires the commitment to allow each other to be and control themselves however they choose. Children who feel respected are socialized and enculturated into expecting that respect is earned on this basis. They are more interested in earning the respect of those they encounter in life. As they understand the requirements for genuine respect, they are less likely to be interested in domination-based

---

[41] Read "Fifty Ways to Leave Leviathan" by Jeffrey Tucker and Max Borders at http://skyler.link/fee50lev

relationships. This bodes well for building a culture of liberty.

Many homeschoolers practice aspects of unschooling, but unfortunately homeschooling can be just as incompatible toward building a culture of liberty as is schooling. All compulsory means of education should be abandoned if the goal is liberty.[42] Children won't grow up understanding and demanding freedom if they don't experience it in their formative years. A radical unschooling home - and to a lesser extent attending a Sudbury Valley-modeled democratic school - is the best environment to building and maintaining a culture of liberty.[43]

---

[42] Read "The Right to Control One's Learning" by John Holt at http://skyler.link/evclearning
[43] Read "Children Educate Themselves" by Peter Gray at http://skyler.link/ptpgcet4

5 AGORISM

"Agorism is a libertarian social philosophy that advocates creating a society in which all relations between people are voluntary exchanges by means of counter-economics, thus engaging in a manner with aspects of peaceful revolution." So says Wikipedia.[44] What is counter-economics? According to the father of Agorism, Samuel Konkin, "the study or practice of all peaceful human action which is forbidden by the State."[45] I think agorism is a much broader concept and practice than was

---

[44] See the Wikipedia entry for "Agorism" at http://skyler.link/wikiagorism

[45] See the Wikipedia entry for "Counter Economics" at http://skyler.link/wikicntrecon

ever suggested by Konkin, and a necessary foundation to building a culture of liberty.

Education

Josef Stalin, the anti-libertarian Russian despot said that "Ideas are more powerful than guns. We would not let our enemies have guns, why should we let them have ideas?" Indeed. Ideas are a powerful thing. So much so that governments everywhere have set up schools and, with very few exceptions, require attendance. Today we see governments encouraging parents to send their little ones to school earlier and earlier.[46] And what ideas are children taught in school? Along with everything I covered in Chapter 3, they're taught pro-government ideas, beginning with the coercively required recital every morning of the "Pledge of Allegiance" to the nation-state (at least in the US). When parents choose radical unschooling over government schools, they are entering the *agora* (Greek for "open space") and providing a foundation of educational freedom and exploration, where no idea is prohibited, for their children. Some of the more dangerous ideas learned in the agora, other than attachment

---

[46] See the Wikipedia entry for "Head Start Program" at http://skyler.link/wikiheadstart

parenting and radical unschooling, from the government's point of view, are as follows.

Governance vs. the State

Once someone decides that they value liberty, the often begin studying liberty. For me, I began valuing liberty after I learned a bit of economics.[47] Once I understood the disastrous effects of government interventions in the market, I wanted to know more about getting rid of those interventions, about increasing liberty. As I followed this path, it became clearer to me the nature of government, of the state. I've always valued and still value "governance", what Mark Bevir defines as "all processes of governing, whether undertaken by a government [the state], market or network, whether over a family, tribe, formal or informal organization or territory and whether through laws, norms, power or language."[48] So, isn't that the state? Not exactly.

The state is a non-contractual monopoly of governance (the legal use of force) within a defined

---

[47] Read "My Road to Liberty Went Through Economics" by the author at http://skyler.link/evcmyroad

[48] See the Wikipedia entry on "Governance" at http://skyler.link/wikigovernance

territorial boundary.[49] As it's non-contractual, it was founded and maintained on the basis of conquest, not consent. Therefore, the state is a violation of liberty. And every state, every government, that exists today was founded and is maintained in this same way.[50] Once I discovered this, I began opposing the existence of the state because of the conflicts it presented to my values (consent, legitimacy, morality, liberty, peace). I became a voluntaryist, one who opposes the ideas that some people may rule over others; that might makes right; that it's morally or philosophically right to initiation coercion against the innocent.[51]

State Law is Mere Risk

Once the state is understood, how should one view its laws? The agorist, understanding the illegitimate nature of the state, views its laws as a matter of risk. One is not honor-bound to obey illegitimate state law other than where its violation puts the realization of one's values at risk. The state is simply a larger and better organized

---

[49] Read "Government vs. the State, Redux" by the author at http://skyler.link/evcgovvsstate

[50] Read "The Anatomy of the State" by Murray Rothbard at http://skyler.link/evcanatomy

[51] Read "The Ethics of Voluntaryism" by the author at http://skyler.link/evcethics

criminal syndicate. We go about our lives mitigating such risks as natural disasters, accidents, and petty crime. State laws are merely one more type of risk to be mitigated.[52] We pay our taxes not because paying taxes is the good and moral thing to do, but because if we don't, we risk being thrown in the rape factory that is prison, or worse.[53] The less risky it is to violate a given state law, the agorist will do so without shame, all in the hope that the more this occurs the greater the chance the given law will be seen as obsolete and remain unenforced.[54] The more laws that agorist activity can make obsolete, the better circumstances are for building a culture of liberty, which leads us to entrepreneurship.

Entrepreneurship

An entrepreneur is someone who operates a business, taking on greater than normal financial risk. In order to succeed, they must successfully anticipate consumer demand and offer the agreeably-priced supply. This takes, among other

---

[52] Read "The Law is Mere Risk" by the author at http://skyler.link/evclawrisk

[53] Read "When Does Law Become Criminal?" by the author at http://skyler.link/evclawcriminal

[54] Read "Agorist Living" by Nicholas Hooton at http://skyler.link/evcagoristliving

things, creativity, inventiveness, and foresight. It also takes capital and a willingness to jump through any number of legal hurdles, some areas more onerous than others. Entrepreneurs, in my opinion, are the heroes of the world.[55] They've brought to the masses the printing press, the automobile, the computer, the Internet[56], and every other amazing thing we take for granted these days. In short, they make us more powerful, and often that power is great enough to increase our liberties.

Entrepreneurs continue to make us more powerful and help us get what we want, and today we see things like cryptocurrencies, decentralized web commerce, and encrypted peer-to-peer networks, each of which are making great strides in battling meddlesome government.[57] The more entrepreneurial activity the better, in my opinion. A relevant fact, a far higher percentage of radical

---

[55] Read "The Entrepreneur on the Heroic Journey" by Dwight Lee and Candace Allen at http://skyler.link/feeheroic

[56] Listen to "Ep. 333 Could There Have Been an Internet Without the State?" from the Tom Woods Show at http://skyler.link/tw333internet

[57] See the Wikipedia entries on "Cryptocurrency" at http://skyler.link/wikicryptocurrency, "OpenBazaar" at http://skyler.link/wikiopenbazaar, "Peer-to-peer" at http://skyler.link/wikip2p

unschoolers become entrepreneurs than their schooled or homeschooled counterparts.[58]

Spreading libertarian ideas, making government laws obsolete, and building the products and services that will give greater and greater power to the masses is what agorism is all about. These things are what's keeping liberty alive today. If we ever want a free society, we must each find ways to contribute in these areas. Start by raising your children in liberty, in the agora. In the next and final chapter of this booklet, I'll explore how moral outrage is developed and why it's necessary in building a culture of liberty.

---

[58] Read "Survey of Grown Unschoolers" by Peter Gray at http://skyler.link/ptpgsgu3

6 MORAL OUTRAGE

Here we are at the conclusion of this booklet. I began by defining several important concepts, each of which I've used here and there, except for moral outrage. (Alright, I used it once.) That is the topic of this final chapter, and the culmination of my thesis on how to build a culture of liberty. Let's go.

What is Moral Outrage?

Let me share once again the definition I offered in Chapter 1:

> "Moral outrage *is a feeling of disgust and/or anger* "to infringements or transgressions on what people perceive to be the immunities they, or others with whom they identify, can expect on the basis of their rights

and privileges and what they understand to be their reasonable expectations regarding the behavior of others." One's socialization will determine what is considered the immunities, rights, and privileges of different groups or classes of people, their violation of which produces the feeling of moral outrage. As it stands, the possibility of moral outrage is a result of one's socialization and enculturation."

Where can we see this today? Here's one example: Americans grow up socialized in government schools and raised by parents and grandparents who were socialized in government schools and possibly served in the military or in a public capacity or is close to someone who did. So, what sort of response is given to someone making a show of burning an American flag? Moral outrage (disgust and anger), because most Americans were socialized and enculturated to hold the American flag and its ideals as not only good and true, but *sacred*. Non-Americans, who weren't socialized and enculturated to revere the American flag feel no such particular outrage. As is obvious, how one is socialized and enculturated determines when and why one feels moral outrage.[59] Let us explore the

---

[59] Read "Whence Cometh Moral Outrage?" by the author at http://skyler.link/evcmoraloutrage

relevance of moral outrage as it concerns the topic explored in each preceding chapter.

Parenting

How children are treated by their parents sets them up to expect certain types of treatments by others. When they are treated in contrary ways, they'll experience moral outrage. If a child's self-ownership is respected, meaning that he's not handled against his will, and he's given honest knowledge and wisdom, then he'll be far less likely to tolerate others violating his self-ownership or dealing with him dishonestly. I see this all the time in children whose rights have been respected by their parents, primarily in my own. They're more assertive of their boundaries and not afraid to stand up for themselves. And more, they empathize with others whose rights are being violated. They experience these violations as their own and the result is moral outrage.

Schooling

How does schooling socialize and enculturate children? And how likely are children to feel moral outrage at the anti-liberty practices found in and out of school, during and after they've left? As already explained, the intent of modern schooling is the production of a conforming and compliant citizenry. Schooling ensures that children are socialized and enculturated *not* to feel moral outrage toward statist, anti-liberty practices like regimentation, deference to authority, and thought-policing. The requisite culture of liberty for a free society *cannot* be built on a foundation of schooling (compulsory education).

Radical Unschooling

When those who are committed to achieving a free society abandon schooling in lieu of the only alternative, radical unschooling (non-compulsory education), they establish an important foundation for increasing the chances of moral outrage toward anti-liberty practices. Children quickly come to expect freedom when experiencing freedom is the norm. When this expectation is unrealized, they'll get confused and angry. They've been allowed to do as they please, and now suddenly someone with more power is telling them they can't. They at first expect a good reason, and failing that their confusion and anger is likely to become full blown moral outrage, at least until their denier of freedom asserts himself as capable of hurting them. They then become resentful, which resentment may one day become violent. My point is, it becomes very difficult and costly to deny children their freedom once they've been allowed to experience it, like anyone else. Ensuring our children experience freedom this early and for as long as possible will create adults who are far more likely to expect and demand freedom.

Agorism

As I expanded my worldview and understanding of economics, philosophy, and so forth, I began feeling a higher degree of moral outrage toward those who forcefully interfere in the lives of others. Education and free thought are a big part of the agora. Likewise, as one engages in peaceful trade, viewing government-made law as just another risk to be mitigated, any increase to that risk can - either as the law expands or as one's trade networks expand - cause a feeling of moral outrage induced by the stress of mitigating such a risk. This can be a healthy feeling as stress is often a catalyst for creative thinking and the development of solutions to overcome the risk. The culture of liberty is then expanded as others adopt and innovate on the solutions discovered.

Here are we at the end. I've written this booklet to provide a way forward for those who value and desire to live in a free society. Unlike others who value liberty, I do not believe that a free society can be achieved through violent revolution. A free society can only result and be maintained on the basis of a culture of liberty, and cultures are the result of socialization, enculturation, and education. As such, I do not believe that a free society and its culture of liberty will remain while parents use either physical or social coercion against their children. Violence in the home teaches domination, not cooperation, nor the equality of liberty and power.[60] Arguably, the home is our greatest sphere of control. We are around our families constantly, and how we behave in relation to them will determine our chances of ever enjoying complete liberty, peace, and prosperity. If you, like me, value these things, then your very first commitment *must* be to raise your children in a culture of liberty and peace. They deserve it, and you deserve it. Godspeed!

---

[60] Read "Liberty: The Other Equality" by Roderick Long at http://skyler.link/feelibertyequality

FURTHER READING

An Agorist Primer, Samuel Konkin III
Basic Economics, Thomas Sowell
Economics in One Lesson, Henry Hazlitt
Education: Free and Compulsory, Murray Rothbard
Free to Learn, Peter Gray
Natural Born Learners, edited by B. E. Ekoko
Nonviolent Communication, Marshall Rosenberg
Parenting a Free Child, Rue Kream
Parenting Effectiveness Training, Thomas Gordon
Parenting for a Peaceful World, Robin Grille
Playful Parenting, Lawrence Cohen
Punished by Rewards, Alfie Kohn
The Problem of Political Authority, M. Huemer
Unconditional Parenting, by Alfie Kohn
Weapons of Mass Instruction, John Taylor Gatto

ABOUT THE AUTHOR

Skyler J. Collins lives with his beautiful wife and three wonderful children in Salt Lake City, Utah. He's a voluntaryist and radical unschooler. He enjoys reading, writing, and podcasting about anything on liberty, economics, philosophy, religion, science, health, and childhood development. He and his wife are committed to raising their children in peace and love, exploring the world with them, and showing them how to deal with others respectfully, and enjoy their freedom responsibly. He is the founder of Everything-Voluntary.com. His websites also include skylerjcollins.com, LibertySearch.info, and LargePrintLiberty.com.